# *Whispers*
## *from the*
# *Heart*

**A Journey from Unbelief
Into God's Amazing Grace**

**By**

**Diane Wise**

First published by AuthorHouse 04/15/04

ISBN: 1-4140-1293-4 (e-book)
ISBN: 1-4184-3803-0 (Paperback)
ISBN: 1-4184-3802-2 (Dust Jacket)

Library of Congress Control Number: 2003097252

This book is printed on acid free paper.

Printed in the United States of America
Bloomington, IN

**All scripture quotations in this book are from
The King James Version of the Bible (KJV)**

In memory
of
Jason Tully Wise
1970—2003

Dedicated to

My loving husband Bill, whom I adore.
My cherished son Mark, trustworthy and kind.
My beautiful daughter-in-law in Christ, Sheryl.
My heartstrings, Hamilton and Emmie Ruth.

The sons Jason
loved so dearly,
Tully L. Wise and Oakley A. Wise.

A special aunt and uncle
Ginger and Dan Brannock.

To my dear friends at
Wise Oil & Fuel, Inc.
for their love and support.

A special thank you to Amy Redmond
and Sheryl Wise, without their expertise
this would not be in print.

# Contents

# Foreword

This journey began at a small church in a sleepy little town on the Eastern Shore of Maryland. A revival was being held. Reverend Claypool was preaching. I cannot tell you about the sermon. I can tell you he met me at the altar. He told me to ask Jesus into my heart and to tell Him I wanted to receive all He had to offer. In an instant, one heartbeat of time, I was transformed. Now I am a sinner saved by God's amazing grace.

# Introduction

My beginning was humble
now I am a child of the King.

A cot was my resting place
now I am revived in my Savior's arms.

Heaven was not a word I used frequently
heaven was a place of unbelief for me.

Tragedy came.
My husband needed a miracle.

It was a June day
clouds of purest white
the sky a cerulean blue.

I looked upward and spoke
life changing words.

God if You exist
in a place I cannot see
I am unworthy to pray.

Head down I walked away
gripped by ice-cold fear
of losing someone
I held so dear.

In recognition of sin
He began to reveal Himself to me.

Now I see a place before unseen.

My husband suffered
a fourth degree electrical burn.
I heard his death rattles.
The body fluids had shifted
and he was unconscious.

He was transported by helicopter to
a burn center two hours away.
It would be seventy-two hours
before they would know
if he would live or die.
This occurred on Saturday at noon.
Sunday passed and Monday
at three in the afternoon
he was back home in his office!

Twelve years later
he is alive and well.
He is minus his thumb
but in the scheme of things
that truly is a miracle.

Thank God, I know Him
as Savior and friend.

Tragedy came again
in the form of death
to our thirty-two year old son.
He was killed in an auto accident.

Now the Lord is leading us through
this garden of grief.

# Salvation

# His

I always want to remember,
The sacrifices of praise to my
Lord and Savior given to me
By the Holy Ghost.

I said, "Lord, I have
Made you my Master."

He said, "No I have
Made you My slave."

*Diane Wise*

# My Prayer

God of mercy and grace
Lord, Your daily walk
With me is my prayer.
May Your blessed Holy Spirit
Always be there.

God I surrender my torments
From which I cannot free myself.

In faith and in trust
I know You will take them
And give peace and contentment
Such as I have never known.

Hebrews 11:6c
*He is a rewarder of them*
*that diligently seek him.*

# Rags to Riches

Upon these pages
I bare my soul.
God of the ages
Made me whole.

To show you my heart
From where I came
If you carry a burden
Or the guilt of shame,

Call on the Great I Am
He is Jehovah He is here,
Living water to cleanse,
Living water to refresh and renew.

What He has done for me
He will do for you.
He is Jehovah
God of the ages.

Psalm 34:18
*The LORD is nigh unto them
that are of a broken heart; and
saveth such as be of a contrite spirit.*

# Salvation

I thank You Father God
You looked down from
Your heavenly home
You saw me
Wandering lost and alone.

In Your mercy,
You gave me grace
To save me from
My wretched fate.

How I want to know Thee
To see Thy face
To hear Thy voice as
I wander the pathways
Of life to be enabled
Always to make the right choice.

I thank You Father
For the love and strength
You send from above,
For my Savior Jesus,
My Lord and first love.

Psalm 102:19, 20
*For he hath looked down*
*from the height of his sanctuary*
*from heaven*
*did the LORD behold the earth;*
*To hear the groaning of the prisoner;*
*to loose those that are appointed to death.*

# The Lamb

Jesus saved my soul
He hung, He bled
To make me whole.

He sent His Spirit
To guide my way,
To keep me safe
By night and by day.

Hallelujah to the Lamb,
Hallelujah for Him I stand.

Isaiah 53:5
*But he was wounded for our transgressions,*
*He was bruised for our iniquities:*

Isaiah 58:11a
*And the LORD shall guide thee continually.*

# Love

O how I love Thee
Lord, how I love Thee

For mending my broken heart
For saving my lost soul;

Seeking always to find
Favor in Your sight,

Praising You
Loving You
For Your mercy
And Your might.

My Lord how I love Thee.

Exodus 15:2a
*The LORD is my strength and song,*
*and he is become my salvation.*

# Bless Him

Father God, I bless You.
I bless Your holy name.

Thank You for Jesus
He bled and He died.
He covered all our shame.

I seek Thy counsel;
A place at the foot of Thy throne,
Seeking God-given wisdom
To be a light to lead
The lost toward home.

Clothe me with humbleness,
Goodness and great love
So all who see may see
A light from above.

Thank You for being my Father.
Thank You for Your Son.
Thank You for the Comforter,
He makes us one.

To God be the glory.

Matthew 5:16
*Let your light so shine before men,
that they may see your good works, and
glorify your Father which is in heaven.*

# Near Him

His presence,
His glorious presence
Comes not from naught.

His being near
Is the blessing
That is sought.

Psalm 16:11
*Thou wilt shew me the path of life:*
*in thy presence is fullness of joy;*
*at thy right hand*
*there are pleasures for evermore.*

# Are You There

Are you there mother?
Father where are you?
Are you there sister?
Brother where are you?
O child of mine where will you go?

Do you know the Father?
Do you know the Son?
Did you feel the warmth and cleansing
Of His blood shed in pain?

There is a hereafter
A place of love, joy and laughter
There is another of burning fire and pain.
Where will you go?

Call on the name of Jesus
To save and deliver.
He will be your friend
For an eternity that has no end.

Call on Him,
Seek Him today.
He will show you the way.
Where will you go?

Acts 2:21
*And it shall come to pass,*
*that whosoever shall call*
*on the name of the Lord*
*shall be saved.*

# His Face

I imagine Your face
As You hung upon the cross
That crucifixion day,

Upturned toward the Father
From whom You felt so faraway.

With beard that was plucked
Flesh that was torn
Blood pouring from Your veins
Your body wrenched in livid pain.

Lamb of God I worship You.
You were slain You bled for me
You saw my face
When You hung on that tree.

I wait in anticipation for that day
Come Lord Jesus rapture me away.


Isaiah 53:5
*But he was wounded for our transgressions,*
*he was bruised for our iniquities:*
*the chastisement of our peace was upon him;*
*and with his stripes we are healed.*

# My Rock

Thank You Lord
For saving my soul.

Thank You Lord
For making me whole.

Thank You Lord
For picking me up,
When I was down.

Thank You Lord
For planting my feet
On solid ground.

I thank You Lord.


Psalm 145:14
*The LORD upholdeth all that fall,*
*and raiseth up all that are bowed down.*

# Illumination

Let the world see
Your light in me.
Lord, You fill my soul.
Where once there was a void,
Your presence makes me whole.

Let all who roam the earth today
In darkness blinded
They cannot see,
Illuminate their path, Lord,
That they might come to Thee.

If they are homeless without a friend,
You will be their shelter, their companion.
If there is no food upon their table
You will be their bread, their provider.
If their garments are tattered and torn,
Your blood will cover and keep them warm.

Fill them Lord
Light their way
Turn their darkness
Into day.

Luke 12:22, 23, 24
*And he said unto his disciples,*
*Therefore I say unto you, Take no thought for your life,*
*what ye shall eat; neither for the body, what ye shall put on.*
*The life is more than meat, and*
*the body is more than raiment.*
*Consider the ravens: for they neither sow nor reap;*
*which neither have storehouse nor barn; and God feedeth them:*
*how much more are ye better than the fowls?*

# Searching

Everywhere I turn,
I see eyes darting to and fro
They are searching
For what they do not know.

Feet are running
Here, there and everywhere
With no place to go.
They are searching
For what they do not know.

There is a space
A void they cannot fill.
Eyes are darting.
Feet are running.
Searching.

They are searching
For another thrill
Another thing
They are seeking to fill
That emptiness that has no name.

He is there.
They cannot see Him.
What a shame.

He has a name it is Jesus;
His arms are open wide,
Waiting to receive them.

He has been there all the time.
They cannot see Him.
What a shame they do not know
If they run into His arms,
They will feel Him.

We must go and tell them.
They can stop searching.
For He will never leave them.
Then and only then,
Will all be well with their souls.


Daniel 12:3, 4
*And they that be wise*
*shall shine as the brightness*
*of the firmament; and they that*
*turn many to righteousness*
*as the stars for ever and ever.*
*But thou, O Daniel, shut up the words,*
*and seal the book, even to the time*
*of the end: many shall run to and fro,*
*and knowledge shall be increased.*

# Growth & Trust

# Rope of Hope

My Lord and my
God, I know not
What tomorrow may bring.

I only know
I need Thee
To carry me
Through all things.

'Tis Thy love and
Thy sustaining strength
That gives me
That extra measure
When my rope
Has reached its length.

In the deep of
The valley
Or the mountain peak
From Your living fountain flows
Hope, Love and Peace.

Christ Jesus I praise Thee.

Isaiah 30:15c
*In quietness and in confidence
shall be your strength.*

# His Call

I heard my Savior calling,
Calling unto me
I cried, "sweet Jesus"
As I fell upon my knees.

He said, "Let me use you
Surrender your will.

Go into the world
Find the broken hearted and the ill.
Tell them of My healing
Of My comforting embrace.

Point the way to heaven
Tell them of My grace."

Call on the name of Jesus
He will be your friend.
Open your heart's door
Invite Him to come in.

He will I promise,
He loves you too.

Thank You, King Jesus,
I belong to You.


Psalm 147:3
*He healeth the broken in heart,*
*and bindeth up their wounds.*

# My Grace

Father God, we ask You to
Bless the bread as we break it
That it will nourish our
Physical bodies.

Lord, we ask You to sustain us
Spiritually with the Living Bread,
The word of God and
The blood of the Lamb.

Father, we love You.
We thank You, You are
Our Jehovah-Jireh in all things.

In His Name
Amen

John 6:50, 51
*This is the bread*
*which cometh down from heaven,*
*that a man may eat thereof and not die.*
*I am the living bread which*
*came down from heaven:*
*if any man eat of this bread,*
*he shall live for ever:*
*and the bread that I will give is my flesh,*
*which I give for the life of the world.*

# My Earthly Father

I never had an earthly father
To love me and teach me.

I am so thankful I have
A heavenly Father to teach
Me and instruct me in the
Way I should go.
I am so thankful.

He guides me with His eye, He truly does.
He is always right. He is never wrong.
I am so thankful. I love Him so.

Looking back, I can see
My stepfather truly loved me,
In his own way.
I hope that in heaven I see him.
There we will embrace.

Anger is a dark drape,
Making it difficult
For the light of love
To penetrate.


Psalm 32: 8
*I will instruct thee and teach thee
in the way which thou shalt go:
I will guide thee with mine eye.*

# Our Guide

Thank You Lord
For allowing me
To help someone today.

Thank You Lord
For Your special way.

You touch our heart;
You speak to our mind.
You are our guide
As we go our way.

Thank You Lord
For direction sent.
As ears, hear Lord
Instill in us
A desire to repent.

Thank You Lord
For blessing us
In everyway.

Psalm 48:14b
*He will be our guide*
*even unto death.*

# His Hand

He reached His hand
He touched me.
He spread His arms
He held me.
He filled my heart
With love for Him.

He lets me know
I am His own.
He will hold me close
I will not roam.
I am His.

He can transform
A cloudy day
A valley, O so deep.
With His love and strength
He imparts peace.

When the new day
Dawns bright
With skies blue,
The butterflies flying
The birds singing

He carries you still
Upon His wing.
Let your heart sing.
He is Lord
His name is Jesus.

Deuteronomy 33:27a
*The eternal God is thy refuge,*
*and underneath are the everlasting arms.*

# Stepping Stones

In the night upon my bed,
Tears of gratitude were shed.
As I turned and looked behind,
I then knew,
He had been there all the time.

What I viewed as tragedies,
He used for stepping-stones,
For you see, I was on the path
Leading away from the throne.

In all things great and small,
He was there in the midst of it all.
In the dark of night or the bright of day,
There need be neither fear nor anxiety.

My Lord and Savior,
Will guide my way
Toward the promise
Of that glorious day.

I praise Him and thank Him for grace.
You see I did not know Him
Only of Him
There is a vast difference
Yet He did not give up on me.

Proverbs 29:25b
*Whoso putteth his trust in the LORD shall be safe.*

# Everything

You are everything.
You are the world to me.
You make my heart sing.
You are my everything.

Within Your embrace,
I rest assured I am safe.

You promised angels all around.
You keep me safe from all harm.
You are a haven from the storm.
You are the world to me.

Your presence is my desire.
Your manifestation is my plea.

Thank You, Savior, from my heart.
You are everything to me.

John 14:21
*He that hath my commandments,*
*and keepeth them, he it is that loveth me:*
*and he that loveth me*
*shall be loved of my Father,*
*and I will love him,*
*and will manifest to him.*

## Thank You Note

I went to my Lord
In prayer today,
Not with a need
Or stumbling blocks
In my way.

Simply, I had something
I needed to say.
I wanted to thank Him
For hearing my prayers.
I wanted to love and praise Him
For answers He has shared.

Peace like a flood,
Washed over me.
Joy welled up
In my soul.

It brought tears
Upon my cheeks,
Just to know
His love is so deep.

If there is one
Of you today,
Who needs an answer
Along your way,

Take it to Him,
In prayer,
And you will see
How much He cares.

He is waiting.

Psalm 37:4
*Delight thyself also in the LORD; and he shall*
*give thee the desires of thine heart.*

# Treasure

Before I came to know
My friend,
Jesus, He is called by men,

I believed I had attained it all:
Worldly wealth, silver and gold.
Alas, in truth, I had nothing
My storehouses were bare and cold.
I was too blind to see.

When heaven's bells rang
And the angels sang
I did not hear.
You see things of this earth
Are what I held dear.

Then one glorious day
He revealed Himself to me.
O what a Savior is my friend
Jesus, He is called by men.

He travels places in my soul
Where others cannot go.
He instills a peace within,
Jesus, my dearest friend.

If you need someone
To love you without measure,
Give Him your heart
To find your true treasure,
Your dearest friend, Jesus.

He loves you.

Matthew 6:21
*For where your treasure is,
there will your heart be also.*

# Like Him

When I walk, Lord,
I want to walk with You.

When I speak, Lord,
I wish to speak
As You command,
Without malice,
Speaking only love.

At the end of the day,
Knowing I walked Your way,
Then I lie down to sleep,
Resting assured
I will rest in peace.
You will be there too.

Then morning comes,
We start anew
Into another day
Blessed by You.

1 Peter 2:1
*Wherefore laying aside all malice,
and all guile, and hypocrisies,
and envies, and all evil speakings.*

# Unforgiveness

Unforgiveness is death
By another name.
It is unnecessary
And causes so much pain.

If unforgiveness
Lives in your heart,
Hope and peace,
It will destroy.

Unforgiveness;
Death, sickness and disease
Ride on its wings.
Take your resentments, slights,
Hurts by other names
To the King.

Give it to the Lord in prayer.
He will give you
Healing and hope
In place of your despair.

May the blessings of
God be upon you;
May peace live in your heart.

Ephesians 4:32
*And be ye kind one to another,*
*tenderhearted, forgiving one another,*
*even as God for Christ's sake*
*hath forgiven you.*

# Canvas

How could I not know
The Lord's love for me?

One glance at the beauty of a tree
The intricate canopy the leaves weave,
In that, I see God's love for me.

Flowers bright,
Cottontails and bunny trails
Make my world a happy place to be,
In that, I see God's love for me.

Chickadees and bluebirds sing
All the daylong
Until the setting of the sun,
In that, I hear God's love for me.

Then night comes.
We see the stars He hung
There for you and for me.

The canvas of His love,
In that, I see
The God of all creation.

Psalm 104:12
*By them shall the fowls
of the heaven have their habitation
which sing among the branches.*

# His Presence

Wherever you go today,
Wherever you may roam,
I will be there by your side,
You will never be alone.

I love you
I call you My own.

Where the river is wide
The mountain high
I will carry you.
The valley O so deep
I will be there too.

I am Lord
Your hope for tomorrow
Your strength for today.

The very one
You will see in eternity.


Psalm 121:2
*My help cometh from the LORD,*
*which made heaven and earth.*

# Compassion

Be gentle with me please
For I am old as you can see.

Countless tears, He has wiped
As I cried through the night.

When I kneel to pray, I hear
My dear Savior say,

"My child I see you there
Upon your knees in earnest prayer."

That is our hope.
That is our promise.

Psalm 6:9
*The LORD hath heard my supplication;*
*The LORD will receive my prayer.*

# Guiding Angels

Upon my deathbed,
When that day arrives
Though friends and family
May not be by my side,

There will be no fear,
Nor the pain of loneliness.

Your presence will be
My shroud Lord,
As I await the death angels
For my ascension into the clouds.

There will be no tears
Upon my cheeks.

I trust in You Lord
My soul You have
Promised to keep.


Matthew 4:6b
*He shall give his angels
charge concerning thee.*


Revelation 21:7a
*He that overcometh
shall inherit all things.*

# Christmas Blessing

We clasp our hands
We bow our heads

We ask You Father
To bless this bread.

Let us remember
The reason for this season.

The Christ Child, Jesus
Born on Christmas Day
To take our sins away,
So far away so long ago
Yet He is He lives.


Luke 2:9, 10, 11
*And lo, the angel of the Lord came upon them,*
*and the glory of the Lord shone round about them:*
*and they were sore afraid.  And the angel said unto them,*
*Fear not: for, behold, I bring you good tidings of great joy,*
*which shall be to all people.  For unto you is born this day*
*in the city of David a Saviour, which is Christ the Lord.*

# Garden of Grief

# In The Garden

When you lose a child
You must go on.
This walk through
The garden of grief
It seems you walk alone.

The Lord will be there
Your burden to share.
He will repair the canvas
Now torn in two.

In this garden
He has not abandoned you.
He is beside you walking, too.
Lean on Him.

The flowers along the way
Far as the eye can see
First are shaded by clouds,
Keep walking
For in time they become
Sweet memories.

Isaiah 40:31
*But they that wait upon the LORD*
*shall renew their strength;*
*they shall mount up with wings as eagles;*
*they shall run and not be weary;*
*and they shall walk, and not faint.*

# My Child

I prayed for my child
Night and day.

My heart was breaking
For his wayward way.


Acts 16:31
*And they said,*
*Believe on the Lord Jesus Christ,*
*and thou shalt be saved,*
*and thy house.*

# Answered Prayer

After the funeral
The place where Jason lived
Was being emptied,
The Bible I had given him
Years before was found
On his table beside the computer.

# Words

I do not know
If these are poems
Or just words
I need to impart.

For when I write them down,
They seem to ease
My aching heart.

I miss my child
The twinkle in his eye
The smile he wore so well.

I told him of Jesus
I pray he listened.
My sweet child, how I miss him.

# Destination

I wrote a poem today
Sent from heaven above,
To quench the fear
For the destiny of
One so greatly loved.

"I am here I am here
Mother dear I am here.
I am looking over to that shore
Watching heaven's gate.

When you are here, mother dear,
We shall sup at the table
With the Lamb the very One
Who professes to be the great I Am.

If only those
Who are still to come
Could see,
The beauty of all that awaits thee,
The glory and light
Of the Divine,
The sparkle of the crystal sea,
To know beyond a
Shadow of doubt,
He is all He speaks about.

The great I Am
He is
He lives."

Revelation 21:10, 11, 12a
*And he carried me away in the spirit*
*to a great and high mountain,*
*and shewed me that great city,*
*the holy Jerusalem.*

# Ultimate Grief

I do not know you
I do know your pain.

I hear your heart's cry
You see mine is the same.

Circumstances may differ
When you lose a child.
However, the loss of a child is
Pain, heart-wrenching pain.

Praise the Lord
Angels carried them away.
To that land of wonder,
We cannot see.

Then one day
When you arrive
You will hear your child say,
"Mommy, Daddy come play with me."

And the games and the joy
Will be without end!

Isaiah 14:3a
*The LORD shall give thee rest from thy sorrow.*

This was written for the mother of a three-year-old child.

# My God

My God,
I know You are alive
I know You live.
I feel You, I hear You,
When You whisper
To my heart.

Your spirit, O God
Like a sweet gentle wind
Brushes over my soul,
When the pain and the sorrow
Are too great to be told.

My heart needs repair.
Sweep over me, Lord,
Come sweet gentle wind
Remove my despair.

When the moment has passed
I am hopeful again,
One day as You promise
In heaven, I shall reign.
There will be no more pain.


Revelation 21:4
*And God shall wipe away*
*all tears from their eyes;*
*and there shall be no death,*
*neither sorrow, nor crying,*
*neither shall there be any more pain:*
*for the former things are passed away.*

# Grace Lord

My cry is for grace, Lord,
God-given grace
For this mountain
I must climb.

Grace, Father,
To heal this broken
Heart of mine.

Grace, God's grace.
My gaze no longer rests
Upon his smiling face,
For you see he departed
This earthly place.

A place where
Grace is everyday
And love is the only way.

Now I am left behind.
However, one day I will be over
This mountain of mine.

I, too, will be there
At the Master's table
Without one care.

If I go first,
I will watch for you
I will save you a place
At the table, too.

He has a feast prepared
Waiting for all who love Him.
I will see you there.


1 Peter 5:10
*But the God of all grace, who hath called us*
*unto his eternal glory by Christ Jesus,*
*after that ye have suffered a while,*
*make you prefect, stablish, strengthen, settle you.*

# One Star

Night after night,
I would go to the window to see
If my Lord had a sign for me.

The night was dark and dreary
A cloud laden sky rolled by,
Nevertheless, His mercy shines,
Grace from this God of mine.

One star
In the dark night.
One star shining bright,
Only one.

It was a message sent just for me.
My Lord Jesus
Heard my plea,
One star, only one
In the dark night.

I left my watching place
Something called me back to see.
It was still there,
One star shining brilliantly.

How could I ever doubt
He sent that star to me?

What a God You are
The God that can send
One brilliant star.

That is grace, truly amazing grace.

Amos 5:8a
*Seek him that maketh
the seven stars and Orion,
and turneth the shadow of death into the morning,
and maketh the day dark with night.*

# Lilies

When I see this misery,
My heart is torn
I want to run from the storm,

Straight into His embrace
To walk the fields of grace
Joy in each bounding step,

Staying there
Until the sky is clear
The storm passed.

Even then, I remain
In that special place
Only the Lord can provide.
That special place,
There by His side,

Sheltered from the storms
Of life,
There where the lilies grow.

Isaiah 26:3, 4
*Thou wilt keep him*
*in perfect peace*
*whose mind is stayed on thee:*
*because he trusteth in thee.*

# Heartstring

To one of my heartstrings,

I could not understand
Your anger,
At times I felt directed at me.

Now I understand it well
A broken heart trying to mend.
Then I just could not comprehend.

Forgive me please
For now I do
My heart is broken too.

From here we shall move
To a higher plane

A forever friendship
Bound by
Pangs of pain.

Then one day
It will be Christmas again,
Family gathered as in times gone by.

This time
We will be rejoicing with
The Bright Morning Star
And those who are waiting
For you and for me.

John 15:12
*This is my commandment,*
*That ye love one another, as I have loved you.*

# Passageway

A friend called today
In search of scripture to read.
Her sister had
Just passed away you see.

Death was on her mind.
Her loved one
Body wasted and diseased
Died cradled in her arms.

She had chosen death
As the topic to read
To those gathered there
For the final farewell.

I reminded her
Death is but
A passageway
To life beyond.

Grave clothes discarded here
Exchanged for a garment
Of purest white,
Prepared by the Master's hand.

Death is not the end
It is the entrance
To the passageway
And the splendor,
Beyond what mortal minds
Can comprehend.

Revelation 3:5
*He that overcometh, the same shall be clothed*
*in white raiment; and I will not blot out his name*
*out of the book of life, but I will confess his name*
*before my Father and before his angels.*

# Safety Net

Lord Jesus,
Hold my hand
When I walk
Upon sinking sand,
That I may not fall
From where I can rise.

You see my heart is torn
Tears are in my eyes.
My loved one departed
He left when you called his name.

Praise God, now
He is on a higher plane.

Grace, Lord,
Grace for tomorrow
Grace to vanquish this sorrow.


Jude 1:24
*Now unto him that is able to keep you from falling,
and to present you faultless before the presence of
his glory with exceeding joy.*

# Somewhere Beyond

Somewhere beyond
Where the eye cannot see
There is a land
Of beauty
Waiting for you and for me.

If I could reach
The outermost part of
My mind
The innermost depth of
My soul

Waiting there for me,
Is beauty beyond
What can be told.

In my mind's eye,
I see
A river of diamonds sparkling
Waiting for me.

I see roses the color of red
The color of blood
My Savior shed.

I see light shining bright
If it shone here, it would blind
You and me.

There in eternity
Is where we will
Just begin to see.

You
The Savior
And me.

Praise God angels will be our guides
To that land beyond the sky
Where the eye cannot see.


Revelation 21:23
*And the city had no need of the sun, neither of the moon, to shine in it:*
*for the glory of God did lighten it, and the Lamb is the light thereof.*

# Goodbye Cloud

I woke today
With a heavy heart.

However, when I seek His face,
He gives me grace.
When I seek Him,
With my whole heart.

Peace He brings
He leaves it there
To lift the burden
Of my cares.

Jesus is His name.
He is the peacemaker.
He is the grace-bringer.
He is the heart-healer.

He truly is the King
He is my Father.

Lamentations 3:22, 23,
*It is of the LORD's mercies*
*that we are not consumed,*
*because his compassions fail not.*
*They are new every morning:*
*great is thy faithfulness.*

# Lord

Lord
Before this tragedy came
I thought I knew You
I even called You friend.

O what a Savior
What a God You are.

You are my heartbeat.
You are the breath I breathe.

Now I know You,
For whom You really are.

You, Lord,
The King of Kings,
The Lord of Lords,
The Rose of Sharon,
The Lily of the Valley,
The Bright Morning Star.

My prayer, Lord,
Are those who know You not
Will come to know You
For the God
You are.

Psalm 34:7, 8,
*The angel of the LORD*
*encampeth round about them*
*that fear him, and delivereth them.*
*O taste and see that the LORD is good:*
*blessed is the man that trusteth in him.*

# Alpha and Omega

He is Lord.
I do not know why
This pain I must bear.

I choose to believe
My Lord saved my
Loved one from despair.

He is the Alpha and the Omega
The beginning and the end.

Perhaps He spared my loved one
From the in-between.

Worship Him
In that place of praise
You shall find your peace.

Revelation 1:8
*I am the Alpha and Omega,*
*the beginning and the ending,*
*saith the Lord,*
*which is, and which was,*
*and which is to come,*
*the Almighty.*

# Choices

I choose
Joy in my Lord
Not despair

To overcome this sorrow,
I now must bear.

He is my light in a dark place.

Let His light shine in your space.

Let His glory in.


2 Peter 1:19
*We have also a more sure word of prophecy;*
*whereunto ye do well that ye take heed,*
*as unto a light that shineth in a dark place,*
*until the day dawn, and the day star arise*
*in your hearts:*

# Understanding

I can understand why
When your heart is
Filled with pain,
You believe you may
Never smile again.
I understand.

Keep walking, continue
Down the road
Around the bend
Across the rocky stream
For what awaits you there
May be another
God-given dream.

He will open doors
And windows too.
Keep walking until you find
What the Lord has in mind.
He will give you
A new dream to pursue.

Isaiah 43:1b, 3a
*Fear not: for I have redeemed thee,*
*I have called thee by thy name;*
*thou art mine;*
*When thou passeth through the waters,*
*I will be with thee; and through the rivers,*
*they shall not overflow thee:*
*when thou walkest through the fire,*
*thou shalt not be burned;*
*neither shall the flame kindle upon thee.*
*For I am the LORD thy God,*
*the Holy One of Israel, thy Saviour:*

# Thank You Jesus

Thank You Jesus
In just one moment,

When I call Your name
You come to me

With healing in Your wings,
You ease the burden of my pain.

I cannot begin to imagine
This walk, this journey here,

Without You Lord being near
As my Savior and my friend.

Isaiah 30:19c
*At the voice of thy cry:*
*when he shall hear it,*
*he will answer thee.*

# Comfort

We each bear our own pain.
Though different it may be
Without it, I could not comfort you,
Nor could you comfort me.

Therefore, in all things
Thankful we must be.

Never forgetting, He suffered for us
And so shall we suffer,
To comfort one another.

Can you imagine being the solitary one
On the face of the earth to endure pain?
No one, no not one,
Would understand you.
How lonely that would be!

2 Corinthians 1:3, 4
*Blessed be God, even the Father of our*
*Lord Jesus Christ,*
*the Father of mercies, and all comfort;*
*Who comforteth us in all our tribulation,*
*that we may be able to comfort*
*them which are in any trouble,*
*by the comfort wherewith*
*we ourselves are comforted of God.*

# Changed

My heart is broken,
My life forever changed.
Yet in this sea of pain,
I am thankful.

God does not leave us
Alone to drown in
Tears and sorrows.

He carries us day by day.
He gives us a hope
For tomorrow

Have no fear
For tomorrow
He will be there too.

# Sweet Whispers

# Jewels

You are God
The creator of the universe.
Earth is Your pleasure,
We are Your possessions.

You pick us up,
You dust us off
Polishing and smoothing
Our rough edges,
Preparing us as Your treasure.

When we have served
Your purpose here,
You will bless us anew.

You will call our name
You will call us home to You.

I am thankful to be
One of Your jewels.

Ephesians 2:10
*For we are his workmanship,*
*created in Christ Jesus unto*
*good works, which God hath*
*before ordained that we*
*should walk in them.*

# Sweet Dreams

Sweet dreams—sweet dreams
I long to be with You
To hear the angels sing,
The beat of holy wings.

I can see—I can see
The beauty of the garden
Where it all began:
The blessed Promised Land.

I cannot wait—I cannot wait
Please open heaven's gate
Let me in.

I can hear—I can hear
The joy from within
It lights my soul
The joy I hear.

I want to stay—I want to stay
In this place of grace
Here now with You
LORD


1 Peter 1:8
*Whom having not seen, ye love;*
*in whom, though now ye see him not,*
*yet believing, ye rejoice with*
*joy unspeakable and full of glory.*

# The Sun

The sun is hiding
Its face today.
I do not see children at play.

Raindrops are falling down
Watering the ground.

In a week or two
We shall see
The faces of flowers new.

Birds splashing
Cleansing themselves
In rain sent by You.

Carpets of green
Mercy and grace
Each place I look
I see Your love for me.


Deuteronomy 28:12a
*The LORD shall open unto thee*
*his good treasure, the heaven to give*
*the rain unto thy land in his season,*
*and to bless all the work of thine hand:*

# Up and Away

Up, up, up,
Away

Beyond the clouds
The brilliant sun
Past the moon
Past the stars,

On into eternity
On my way to heaven,
Where I long to be.

The gate opened wide
When I arrived;
John, Peter and Paul
Welcomed me inside.

They said,
"We are glad you came
Jesus has been calling your name.
Come in
This is where life
Just begins."


2 Peter 3:13
*Nevertheless we, look for new heavens
according to his promise, and a new earth,
wherein dwelleth righteousness.*

# Have You Heard I

As I have traveled time
Through the years,
I have heard many old sayings,
Here are just a few,
I have expanded upon.

Have you heard
That old saying
"Birds of a feather
Flock together"?

Nest with fly with the Savior
You will love the perspective
Of heaven above
The beauty of earth below,
When you fly
On the wings of the Dove.

Have you heard that old saying,
"You become like
The company you keep"?

Spend time with Jesus
It will be time well spent.

Psalm 128:1, 2
*Blessed is every one that feareth*
*The LORD; that walketh in his ways.*
*For thou shalt eat the labour of thine hands.*
*Happy shalt thou be, and it shall be well with thee.*

# Have You Heard II

Have you heard
That old saying,
"A stitch in time saves nine"?

Be still listening,
He is speaking to you.
He is never too early.
He is never too late.
He is always right on time.

Thank You Lord
For speaking to me
Deep in my heart
Where I can hear,
I thank You.

Just then, I heard
My Savior say,
"What makes you think
I am finished with you today.
We have only just begun
This walk together, you and Me,
Into eternity."

Psalm 46:10
*Be still, and know that I am God:*

# Kaleidoscope

Life is like the tide that ebbs and flows.
Emotions run high emotions run low,
Therefore so our lives go.

Life is like the intricacies
The kaleidoscope weaves,
Bits and pieces of broken glass
Many shapes and colors
Tumbling, falling into perfect place.

When viewed through the tunnel
Of mirrored walls,
What beauty the eye beholds
As the broken glass tumbles and falls.

Life is painful, sorrowful
And yet joyful if we allow
The Master to take control.

'Tis beauty we see
Down the mirrored walls.
The intricate patterns
Of broken, colored glass
As it tumbles and falls.

Without the brokenness,
There would be no beauty at all,
Just one piece of solid glass.

Therefore, my friend hold on,
For in the end it will have been
Worth it all.

Just then
I heard His still small voice
Whisper to my heart, "Trust Me".

Put all your trust in Him.
He loves you
He waits for you.


Romans 5:3, 4
*And not only so, but we glory
in tribulations also: knowing that
tribulations worketh patience;
and patience, experience;
and experience, hope:*


2 Corinthians 12:9a
*My grace is sufficient for thee:
for my strength is made
perfect in weakness.*

# Rick St. John
Author of
# Circle of Helmets

A warrior has shared
Pain from the deepest
Depths of his soul.

Praise God,
In the end he has
Shared a story
Before untold.

In the telling of
Anguish and misery
Of names unknown,
They become the face
Of the man next door,
The mother's son
Who returned no more.


Let us thank him.
Let us thank them.

Let us join our hearts in prayer
That when these forgotten war
Heroes close their eyes
Upon their bed,
With God's grace,
They will not look behind,
Only ahead.

Thank you for my liberty.

John 14:27
*Peace I leave with you, my peace I give unto you:*
*not as the world giveth, give I unto you.*
*let not your heart be troubled, neither let it be afraid.*

# Dear One

Lord thank You
For this treasure
Your precious gift to me
My blessed loving husband,
He means the world to me.

Please do not take
Him from me
For then what would life be,
One absent from the other,
What would life be, lonely.

When You call us home
May it be together
Into eternity.

Ephesians 5:25
*Husbands, love your wives,*
*even as Christ also loved the church,*
*and gave himself for it.*

# Mark

Our first-born son
Is more precious
Than gold.

I pray God
Will bless him
And allow him
To grow old.

As he walked
From youth into manhood,
He filled our hearts with pride.

Right choices he made
In honor, he did abide.

A man now wise,
Gentle, quiet and strong.

He built his house
On rock not sinking sand.
His wife, his children
On him, they can depend.

We thank God for him.


Ecclesiastes 2:26
*For God giveth to a man
that is good in his sight wisdom,
and knowledge, and joy.*

# Sheryl

My daughter-in-law
Is as sweet
As she can be.

The Lord picked
A perfect one for me.

The prettiest flower
In the garden,
That is what
Sheryl means to me.

She is a virtuous woman
And I love her.
I thank God for her.


Proverbs 31:10
*Who can find a virtuous woman?*
*For her price is far above rubies.*

# Emmie Ruth

Thinking of my
Sweet granddaughter today
Emmie Ruth is her name,
O what a blessing is she.

When she puts crayon to paper,
Beautiful things you shall see,
Rainbows, hearts,
Colored balloons floating in air
A puppy here, a kitty there.

Sun that shines bright
To grow the flowers she sows,
These are the things that
Warm her heart you know.

In this life what matters most
Are things unseen
Kindness, tenderness, gentleness,
Sweetness, love and hugs.
She possesses all of these.

Wherever the Lord may lead,
She will surely go,
She loves Jesus, I know,
You see she told me so.

Remember
Things unseen matter most,
Plant them in your heart where they can grow
For all to see.

Galatians 5:22, 23
*But the fruit of the spirit is*
*love, joy, peace, longsuffering,*
*gentleness, goodness, faith,*
*meekness, temperance:*
*against such there is no law.*

# Hamilton

When I close my eyes
Hamilton's face I see.
He is my first grandson
He is God's gift to me.

With eyes big,
Brown and bright,
I can tell you
This child is a delight.

Wherever he goes, he turns
Strangers into friends.
You see he gives them
One of his big, wide,
Handsome Hamilton grins!

If he runs into you,
You will be his friend, too.

I hope you have many answers
For he will have questions to ask.
This boy wants to be prepared
For each up and coming task!

Proverbs 15:13a
*A merry heart maketh*
*a cheerful countenance.*

# The Wise Boys
## Jason's two sons

Dear Lord
Tully and Oakley
We see not.

Although
They are in our hearts
And we pray for them a lot.

We ask Your guidance Lord,
Each day as they go and grow
Your perfect way
To them You will show.

When they return to You,
Their journey on earth done,
Jason will be waiting, expectantly
For his two sons.


Ephesians 1:16b, 17
*Making mention of you in my prayers;*
*That the God of our Lord Jesus Christ,*
*the father of glory, may give unto you*
*the spirit of wisdom and revelation*
*in the knowledge of him.*

# Not Perfect Yet

Thank God,
When He beckoned
We answered His call.

To my fellow Christians
One and all.

I have sinned
You have sinned
Therefore, judge me not
Unless I sin again.

God forbid, but if I do
Please come to me
Lovingly lead me back
To where I should be.

Thank you and love to you
In Christ Jesus.

James 5:19, 20
*Brethren, if any of you do err
from the truth, and one convert him;
Let him know, that he which converteth
the sinner from the error of his way
shall save a soul from death,
and shall hide a multitude of sins.*

# Bedchamber

If you are saved and reborn,
You then know and love the Lord.
You are His earthen vessel
He resides within.

If He remains in the parlor
Where guests are received,
Invite Him to the bedchamber
The most intimate place to be.

Yield yourself completely.
He will love and cherish you
Like none other you have ever known.

Ezekiel 16:8
*Now when I passed by thee, and looked upon thee,
behold, thy time was the time of love;
and I spread my skirt over thee,
and covered thy nakedness: yea I swore unto thee,
and entered into a covenant with thee,
saith the Lord God, and thou becamest mine.*

# Tidbits

# Cleansed

My love for Him wells up
It overflows my soul.

His daily cleansing power
Is a wonder to behold.


Isaiah 1:18
*Come now, and let us reason*
*together, saith the LORD:*
*though your sins be as scarlet,*
*they shall be as white as snow;*
*though they be red like crimson,*
*they shall be as wool.*

# El Shaddi

El Shaddi
From on high
He is my sustainer

I feed on Him
I drink Him in
He is LORD.

John 4:14b
*The water that I shall give him*
*shall be in him a well of water*
*springing up into everlasting life.*

# Days

May all our days
Be sunshine filled.

However, when clouds
Roll in and raindrops fall,

We have the assurance
The Lord holds our umbrella

Just as He holds us
In the palm of His hand.


Isaiah 41:10
*Fear thou not; for I am with thee:*
*Be not dismayed; for I am thy God:*
*I will strengthen thee; yea I will help thee*
*With the right hand of my righteousness.*

# Constant Companion

My prayer is the Lord
Will embrace you
As you wake and begin
Your day.

He will watch and guide you
As you go your way.

When night falls
He will hold you and love you
He will chase your loneliness away.

My prayer for widows
And widowers.


Psalm 146:8b
*The LORD raiseth them
that are bowed down.*


Matthew 28:20b
*and, lo, I am with you alway,
even unto the end of the world.*

# Burden Bearer

If you have a problem
Do not give it to
The world to share

With upraised arms
And hope in your heart
Take it to the Lord
In prayer.

Psalm 55:22a
*Cast thy burden upon the LORD,*
*and he shall sustain thee:*

# Mercy

His truth is a treasure
It will make you weep

It is truth you must share
To those in despair.

He is the Healer.
He is the King.

Mercy and grace
To you He will bring.

Romans 10:12b
*The same Lord over all is rich unto
all that call upon him.*

# Dependable

Wait on Me my child
I will be your guide.

Through good days
And bad days
I will walk by your side.

Glory, glory, glory
To the Lord on high.


John 12:26
*If any man serve me, let him follow me;*
*and where I am, there also shall my servant be:*
*if any man serve me, him will my Father honour.*

# Jehovah-Jireh

Jehovah-Jireh
The God of all the ages
You walked upon the sand
So very long ago, yet You are the same God
That holds my hand when I need You so.
Jehovah-Jireh

Most Holy God
You staked Your claim within my heart.
With Your blood, You carved Your name
Now I am forever changed.

To You I surrender my will
Knowing Lord I shall never have
A need You cannot fulfill.


Genesis 22:13, 14a
*And Abraham lifted up his eyes,*
*and looked, and behold behind him*
*a ram caught in a thicket by his horns:*
*and Abraham went and took the ram, and*
*offered him up for a burnt offering*
*in the stead of his son.*
*And Abraham called the name*
*of that place Jehovah-Jireh:*

# Grandeur

My words are limited
I cannot express
The beauty I feel
Awaits me there.

If only I could paint a picture
Of things I cannot see,

It would capture
The grandeur
Of that place
We call eternity.

Revelation 4:3
*And he that sat was to look upon*
*like a jasper and a sardine stone:*
*and there was a rainbow*
*round about the throne,*
*in sight like unto an emerald.*

# Journey

My journey is almost at the end
If I had it to do over again

I would seek my Savior's face
When my journey first began.


Psalm 146:1, 2
*Praise ye the LORD.*
*Praise the LORD O my soul.*
*While I live will I praise the LORD:*
*I will sing praises unto my God*
*while I have any being.*


Proverbs 8:17b
*Those that seek me early*
*shall find me.*

# Silence

A comforting embrace
Speaks a thousand words
Without saying one.

1 Thessalonians 5:11a
*Wherefore comfort yourselves*
*Together, and edify one another.*

# Best Friends

For some time now
I have not been in church,
That place of brick and stone.

In my solitude
I have grown ever so close
To my Lord,
The best of places to be.

Jeremiah 29:13
*And ye shall seek me, and find me,
when ye shall search for me
with all your heart.*

James 4:8a
*Draw nigh to God,
and he will draw
nigh to you.*

# Goodbye

When my time is come,
These parting words I leave behind
For my beloved family.

Please do not
Shed your tears for me.

For at last
I am here
Where I longed
To be,

In His light
Now I see,
No longer in a dimly
Lit mirror,

Rejoicing forevermore.

1 Corinthians 13:12
*For now we see through a glass, darkly;*
*But then face to face:*
*Now I know in part;*
*but then shall I know*
*even as also I am known.*

# About the Author

Diane Wise is a sixty-two year old wife and mother writing her first book. She has been married forty years and had two sons, Mark and Jason. She has been a stay-at-home wife and mom throughout her married life. Her sons grew and married, blessing her with four grandchildren. She had a love for antiques, refinishing and decorating. Now, her first love is the Lord. She first began to journal with her salvation at age fifty-one. Then with the untimely death of her youngest son, she has begun the healing process with these outpourings of comfort from the Lord. Her hope is if you know the Lord you will be blessed as you read, if you know Him not, you will be drawn to Him and if you are grieving for a loved one, you will find a measure of comfort in these whispers from her heart.

CPSIA information can be obtained at www.ICGtesting.com
Printed in the USA
BVOW08*0357041115

425498BV00002B/5/P